AMERICA AT WAR

THE WAR OF 1812
1812–1815

Simon Rose

www.av2books.com

AV² provides enriched content that supplements and complements this book. Weigl's AV² books strive to create inspired learning and engage young minds in a total learning experience.

Your AV² Media Enhanced books come alive with...

Audio
Listen to sections of the book read aloud.

Key Words
Study vocabulary, and complete a matching word activity.

Video
Watch informative video clips.

Quizzes
Test your knowledge.

Embedded Weblinks
Gain additional information for research.

Slide Show
View images and captions, and prepare a presentation.

Try This!
Complete activities and hands-on experiments.

... and much, much more!

Go to www.av2books.com, and enter this book's unique code.

BOOK CODE

F745923

AV² **by Weigl** brings you media enhanced books that support active learning.

Published by AV² by Weigl
350 5th Avenue, 59th Floor
New York, NY 10118

Websites: www.av2books.com   www.weigl.com

Library of Congress Cataloging-in-Publication Data

Rose, Simon.
 The War of 1812 / Simon Rose.
    pages cm. -- (America at war)
 Includes index.
 ISBN 978-1-4896-0516-0 (hardcover : alk. paper) -- ISBN 978-1-4896-0517-7 (softcover : alk. paper) -- ISBN 978-1-4896-0518-4 (ebk.) -- ISBN 978-1-4896-0519-1 (ebk.)
 1. United States--History--War of 1812--Juvenile literature. I. Title.
 E354.R67 2014
 973.5'2--dc23
                          2014017455

Printed in the United States of America in North Mankato, Minnesota
1 2 3 4 5 6 7 8 9 0 18 17 16 15 14

052014
WEP310514

Editor: Heather Kissock
Design: Mandy Christiansen

Photograph Credits
We acknowledge Getty Images, Alamy, Newscom, and Corbis as our primary photo supplier. Canadian War Museum: pages 16T, 16L, 17T, 17L; Dave Pelland/CTMonuments.net: page 43L.

Every reasonable effort has been made to trace ownership and to obtain permission to reprint copyright material. The publishers would be pleased to have any errors or omissions brought to their attention so that they may be corrected in subsequent printings.

CONTENTS

America at War

T he United States is a country that was born out of conflict. The American Revolutionary War was a fight for independence from **colonial rule**. From 1775 to 1783, colonists fought British rule for the right to forge their own destiny. Their commitment to the cause established the country as a fierce and loyal **ally**. When called upon, the United States has always fought bravely to protect its values and way of life.

Some of the battles of the War of 1812 used both army and navy forces. The Battle of Plattsburgh is sometimes called the Battle of Lake Champlain because it was fought both on land and sea.

Since its inception, the United States has been involved in a number of wars and conflicts. These include the War of 1812, the American Civil War, the Mexican-American War, and several battles with American Indians. The United States was also involved in the latter stages of World War I and played a major role in World War II. Since 1945 alone, the United States has taken part in conflicts in Korea, Vietnam, Iraq, and Afghanistan.

No matter how a war ends, it usually leads to changes for both sides of the conflict. On the global scale, borders change, new countries are created, people win their freedom, and **dictators** are deposed. Changes also occur on a national level for almost every country involved.

The United States has experienced great change as a result of war. War has shaped the country's political, economic, and social landscape, making it the country it is today.

Naval battles played a key role in the War of 1812. Control of the Great Lakes, in particular, was considered necessary as they provided both sides with a transportation route for military supplies.

A War Begins

The United States declared independence from Great Britain in 1776, and the war between the two countries ended in 1783. However, relations between Great Britain and the new United States remained strained for a number of reasons. Some of these related to issues that had not been resolved between the two countries after the American Revolutionary War, while others were new causes of dispute.

Since 1803, Great Britain had been at war with France and its leader, Napoleon Bonaparte. The war was waged on battlefields and on the economies of both countries. When France attempted to prevent Europe from trading with Great Britain, the British set up **blockades** that restricted trade between the United States and France. The British Royal Navy also forcibly recruited Americans into its ranks, ignoring protests from the U.S. government.

While the battle went on in Europe, Americans were making efforts to expand the United States by settling the West. They faced British interference on this front as well, as the British were supplying arms to the American Indians who were fighting U.S. expansion. Some American politicians believed that the best way to handle the British high-handedness was to eradicate all British presence in North America. This meant taking control of Canada. They believed that, only by taking firm action, would the United States preserve its national honor.

Prior to becoming the first emperor of France, Napoleon Bonaparte served as a general in the French army. He continued to lead troops into battle throughout the Napoleonic Wars.

The Roots of the War of 1812

TRADE ISSUES

In 1806, Napoleon established the Continental System, which closed all European ports to British ships. In response, the British issued the Orders in Council, which closed European ports to trade unless ships called at a British port first and paid **customs duties**. The British Royal Navy blockaded Europe, and the French declared that any ship following Great Britain's rules would be seized. All of this had a serious effect on U.S. ships trying to trade with Europe. The U.S. government brought in measures to try to protect its trade, but the American economy still suffered.

IMPRESSMENT

Besides blocking U.S. ships from European ports, the British Navy routinely stopped and searched U.S. ships for **deserters**. Sometimes, the British went beyond taking their own sailors back. They also forcibly removed U.S. sailors from their own ships and recruited them into the British Navy in an act called impressment. The United States had fought for its independence from Great Britain, so impressment brought the issue of U.S. **sovereignty** to the forefront. The U.S. government asserted that its citizens could not be forced to fight for Great Britain.

AMERICAN EXPANSION

As more people began moving to the United States, settlements began to extend farther inland. American Indians were displaced as a result of this expansion. This led to conflicts between settlers and American Indians. When the British supplied Shawnee Chief Tecumseh with arms, he promised that he and his allies would help Great Britain if war broke out with the United States. As the number of American Indian raids in settled areas increased, settlers began to complain that the British were inciting the American Indians to prevent westward expansion.

WAR HAWKS

Outraged by the British blockade, the impressment of U.S. citizens, and interference in U.S. expansion plans, a group of politicians called the War Hawks were determined to fight for the country's liberties. They believed that the current government was not taking appropriate actions against Great Britain. By the fall of 1811, these politicians were openly discussing the idea of invading Canada. At the time, Canada had a small population and was only lightly defended by the British. The War Hawks believed that capturing Canada would be easy.

A Second War of Independence

While the War of 1812 had international connections because of the situation in Europe, most of the fighting took place in North America. Neither the United States nor Canada was the size each is today. Therefore, much of the war took place in a very localized area along what is now the international border between New York State and the Canadian provinces of Quebec and Ontario. In fact, most of the War of 1812 was fought in and around Lake Erie.

The map to the right shows the scope of the War of 1812 and the key battles that took place.

Queenston
Heights

Lundy's Lane

Chippawa

Fort Erie

Crysler's Farm

Plattsburg

York

Moraviantown

Battle of
the Thames

Detroit

Frenchtown

Battle of
Lake Erie

Baltimore

Godly
Wood

Bladensburg

Washington

Horseshoe Bend

New Orleans

Fort St. Philip

Legend

British Blockade

United States

British Colonies

Neutral

0   250 Miles

0   250 Kilometers

N

The United States Enters the War

As American Indian attacks continued on the western frontier and the British continued to seize American ships and sailors at sea, some U.S. politicians demanded war. Although Great Britain and the United States had been involved in bitter disputes for several years, neither side was prepared for war in early 1812. Still, some Americans felt that it would not take much effort to capture Canada and that taking possession of the British colony to the north would solve their problems with the British once and for all. The British, on the other hand, did not want to fight a war in North America until they had ended their war against France. The British Parliament voted to **repeal** the Orders in Council and end restrictions on American trade. However, as communications were still very slow in 1812, this news took three weeks to reach the United States. In the meantime, politicians in Washington continued to debate going to war with Great Britain.

A British blockade of U.S. ports began almost immediately upon declaration of war. British ships wasted no time in hampering U.S. ships coming out of places such as Chesapeake Bay, and off the coasts of Maryland and Virginia.

On June 1, 1812, President Madison sent a message to Congress. It detailed the country's grievances against Great Britain, such as the trade issues and impressment of sailors, but did not ask for a formal declaration of war. Three days later, the House of Representatives voted for war. The Senate took longer to debate the issue, as some people tried to restrict the scope of the fighting. The first vote was a deadlock. However, on June 17, the Senate also elected to go to war. The War of 1812 officially began the next day.

James Madison
The Fourth U.S. President

James Madison was born in Virginia, in 1751. He spent his childhood at the family's tobacco plantation at Montpelier. After graduating from the College of New Jersey, Madison entered politics and was elected to the Virginia state legislature in 1776. During the American Revolutionary War, he became a member of the **Continental Congress**, where he worked hard to maintain the unity of the states. After the war, Madison played a leading role at the Constitutional Convention, stressing the need for a strong federal government for the United States.

Madison served in the House of Representatives from 1789 to 1797, where he worked on the Bill of Rights. These 10 amendments to the U.S. Constitution established the rights of all Americans. Madison served as secretary of state under Thomas Jefferson and doubled the size of the country in 1803, when Louisiana was purchased from France. He was elected as president in 1809 and stayed in office until 1817. He died in Virginia in 1836, at the age of 85.

James Madison married Dolley Payne Todd on September 15, 1794. Dolley is credited with reinventing the role of First Lady, giving the U.S. president's wife a clearly defined role within the White House.

Madison is often referred to as the "father of the Constitution" for the role he played in proposing the document's structure and content. The U.S. Constitution was signed on September 17, 1787.

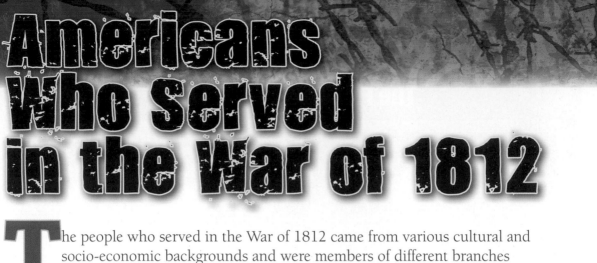

Americans Who Served in the War of 1812

The people who served in the War of 1812 came from various cultural and socio-economic backgrounds and were members of different branches of the country's armed forces. Most were soldiers in the U.S. Army. However, some were recruited from militias. These were forces from individual American states and local communities. Sailors in the U.S. Navy mostly served in the Atlantic Ocean and the Great Lakes, although there were some battles with Royal Navy ships in other parts of the world. Although American Indians usually fought on the side of Great Britain, some groups, such as the Cherokee, were allies of the United States.

Soldiers

In June 1812, the U.S. Army had less than 12,000 men. Approximately 5,000 of these men were recruits, who had only joined the military earlier that year. Even so, this was significantly greater than the 7,000 British and Canadian soldiers to the north. The U.S. government wanted to ensure it had a large fighting force. Plans were quickly made to expand the U.S. Army to 35,000 men. However, it was difficult to get more recruits. The army did not pay well, and few men wanted to volunteer.

Cavalry, or horse-mounted, units fought alongside ground soldiers. They also acted as scouts and messengers.

There were also very few experienced or trained officers when the war began. The existing soldiers may have had experience defending settlements against American Indians, but they knew very little about battlefield tactics. While they quickly learned about firing muskets in battle and making charges with bayonets, the soldiers' lack of military knowledge led to many defeats in the early stages of the war. In the spring of 1814, General Winfield Scott established a training camp at Buffalo. The training the soldiers received there allowed them to defeat the British at the Battle of Chippawa a few months later.

Militia

Militias were not part of the official U.S. Army. They were reserve forces that could be called upon to fight during time of war. When not at war, their job was to maintain law and order in their own communities. The last time the militia units had been called to fight was during the American Revolutionary War, more than 30 years earlier. Most states had not maintained their militia units since that time. The soldiers were untrained and lacked weapons. As a result, the men were ill-prepared to fight in 1812.

Many of the militia soldiers also resisted the call to duty. Once the war began, militia members would sometimes be unwilling to fight or to cross national borders. They believed their main duty was to defend against invasion, not to go on the **offensive**. Militia soldiers often only served for a set time. They went home when their tour of duty was over, even if they were still needed on the field. Army soldiers often perceived the militia to be unreliable as a fighting force because of this.

Militia often performed poorly in battles against the professional and experienced British forces during the war.

Sailors

The U.S. Navy was formed in 1789, but had very few ships in 1812. There were only about 5,000 sailors and 1,000 marines when the war began. However, what the navy lacked in resources, it made up for in experience. Most of the navy's officers were professionally trained, and many of the sailors had fought in the **Barbary War**. Some U.S. sailors had also gained experience when they were forced to serve on Royal Navy ships.

Most of the encounters between American and British ships took place in the North Atlantic. However, U.S. sailors on the *Essex* fought the British in the Pacific before being captured by the Royal Navy off the coast of Chile. The biggest naval battle of the war did not take place at sea. In the Battle of Lake Erie, U.S. sailors on nine ships defeated and captured six Royal Navy ships. Their victory ensured U.S. control of the Great Lakes for the rest of the war.

Some sailors served on U.S. privateer ships. These were private ships that the government hired to attack foreign vessels. One of the best-known privateers of the War of 1812 was Jean Lafitte, who fought during the Battle of New Orleans.

Commodore Oliver Hazard Perry commanded the U.S. Navy during the Battle of Lake Erie and is often referred to as the hero of the battle. When his first ship was destroyed during the battle, he transferred to another ship to continue fighting.

American Indians

Most American Indians allied themselves with the British during the War of 1812. However, there were a few groups that fought for the United States. American Indians played key roles in the battles no matter what side they supported. Besides fighting alongside regular soldiers in battle, they served as scouts, locating enemy positions and helping plan travel routes.

Red Jacket was the leader of the Seneca during the War of 1812. Initially siding with the United States in the war, he removed his warriors from the fighting following the Battle of Chippawa after experiencing excessive losses.

For some American Indians, the War of 1812 was a divisive conflict. Alliances among groups were broken as some American Indians decided to support the British and others sided with the Americans. In the north, the alliance most impacted was the Iroquois Confederacy, an alliance of six American Indian groups. While five of the groups joined the British effort, the Seneca believed that they would gain more by fighting for the Americans. After meeting each other in battle, however, they decided that their alliance meant more to them than the war and withdrew their warriors from both sides.

THE CREEK WAR

In the South, the War of 1812 escalated previous tensions among the Creek Confederacy. Like most American Indian groups, the confederacy felt threatened by U.S. expansion. However, while the Lower Creek decided to remain neutral in the conflict between the British and the Americans, the Upper Creek supported the British plan to halt western expansion. This led to conflict within the confederacy, and a civil war broke out. The Lower Creek called on the U.S. government for help.

By this time, the U.S. Army was already engaged in the War of 1812 and could not spare many troops. The job of quelling the uprising fell to the local militia, led by Andrew Jackson. They joined an American Indian force that included the Lower Creek, Choctaw, and Cherokee warriors. These warriors helped the Americans defeat the Upper Creek at the Battle of Horseshoe Bend in March 1814, and the Creek War was over.

A Soldier's Uniform

HAT
Most soldiers wore a shako as headgear. A shako was a tall, cylindrical cap with a visor. The front of the cap featured a cap badge, which indicated the soldier's **regiment**. Feather plumes extended from the top of the badge. Some shakos also featured a braided cord and tassels.

Soldiers heading to war were equipped with a uniform that they wore while on active duty in the field. Each soldier also had a kit that accompanied the uniform. The kit contained all of the equipment that the soldier was expected to need while away from camp. The soldier carried his gear wherever he went. These are examples of the uniforms and gear worn by U.S. soldiers during the War of 1812.

COAT
Soldiers wore a type of coat called a coatee. Made of wool, the coatee was short at the front but long in the back, typically extending at least halfway to the knees. The style and colors varied between different regiments, but most American coatees were dark blue. The blue coats helped American soldiers distinguish their colleagues from the British soldiers, who mainly wore red coats.

TROUSERS
A soldier's trousers had a high waist. The waistband of the trousers reached to the bottom of the soldier's breastbone and had buttonholes for suspenders. The trousers had a loose-fitting, straight leg. Sometimes, **gaiters** were worn over the trouser bottoms to prevent dirt or stones from getting inside the soldier's shoes. In the summer, soldiers wore white linen or cotton trousers. Winter trousers were made of dark blue wool.

FOOTWEAR

A soldier's shoes were ankle height, with rough leather on the outside. They were tied with laces. The soldier's socks and stockings were made of wool or a mixture of wool and cotton. Socks were worn with half-gaiters, also called spatterdashes. These were ankle-height and made of canvas. They had buttons on the outer edge and a leather strap that passed under the shoe to fasten on the opposite side. Stockings were worn with knee-high gaiters and breeches.

HAVERSACK

The haversack was sometimes referred to as a bread bag. Soldiers carried their cutlery and rations in their haversack. The haversack's linen strap was worn over the soldier's right shoulder so that the sack itself rested on his left hip.

KNAPSACK

A soldier's knapsack was a simple double envelope linen bag. It was painted on the outside to make it waterproof and had leather shoulder straps. The knapsack was used for carrying the soldier's blanket, mess equipment, toiletry articles, and spare shoes and clothing. A strap at the top of the knapsack was used to secure the rolled blanket.

CANTEEN

All soldiers were issued canteens to carry water. Three different types of canteen were in use during the War of 1812. The most common canteen looked like a small wooden barrel. It was painted blue and had the letters "U.S." stenciled on one end. The box-style canteen was also made of wood. To make it waterproof, this canteen was sealed with wax on the inside. The tin canteen was stronger, longer lasting, and easier to repair. All canteens had a carrying strap and were usually placed on top of the soldier's haversack, on his left side.

CARTRIDGE BOX

Soldiers stored their ammunition in their cartridge box. Made of black leather, the box was hung over the soldier's left shoulder so that it rested on his right hip. Inside the cartridge box was a wooden block that held 24 cartridges. The soldier kept extra cartridges, cleaning cloths, and spare flints in a tin tray under the block.

Weapons of War

Most battles during the War of 1812 involved two armies facing each other over a wide distance. They would fire repeatedly at each other from afar before advancing for closer combat. The weapons used had to be suitable for this type of fighting. Cannons and other large guns were used for distance shooting, but smaller weapons were required when fighting hand-to-hand. Both sides relied on muskets, pistols, bayonets, and swords for this part of the battle.

MUSKETS

The majority of U.S. Army soldiers carried the 1795 Springfield Flintlock **Infantry** Musket into battle. The musket was 59 inches (1.5 meters) long and weighed 9 pounds (4.1 kilograms). It fired either a soft lead ball or a combination of one ball and three buckshot. Trained soldiers could fire two to three rounds per minute in battle. The musket's effective range was 100 to 150 yards (91.4 to 137.2 m).

BAYONETS

Soldiers usually attached a bayonet, or knife, to the top of their musket's barrel. The bayonet was used when charging at the enemy or in hand-to-hand combat. When not in use, the bayonet was stored in a scabbard carried on the soldier's shoulder belt.

SWORDS AND SABERS

Soldiers in the War of 1812 had a variety of swords at their disposal. Straight-bladed swords were usually carried by cavalry units, while sabers were usually carried by light **artillery** and **dragoon** units. Most sword blades were 26 to 28 inches (66 to 71.1 centimeters) long. Infantry soldiers used swords while engaging in hand-to-hand combat. Cavalry soldiers swung their sabers at the enemy during charges.

PISTOLS

In addition to a saber, U.S. cavalry units were armed with flintlock pistols. The most common model was the 1805 .54 caliber pistol, which had a 10-inch (25.4-cm) long steel barrel and a curved handle. Cavalry pistols were carried in a holster on the side of the soldier's saddle. Pistols were only effective at close range and were used against other cavalry units or groups of enemy infantry.

CANNONS

Cannons were used to destroy fortifications, soldiers, and horses. They would be moved into place on a wooden carriage pulled by horses and then readied for battle. The most commonly used cannon of the war was the six-pounder, which fired a 6-pound (2.7 kg) roundshot, sometimes referred to as a cannonball. Six-pounders had long barrels to allow them to fire at long range. The gun crew would aim the weapon by looking along the barrel toward the target. The guns were very heavy and recoiled, or rolled back, up to 6 feet (1.8 m) when fired. The gun crew usually comprised strong men able to return the gun to its original position so that the next shot could be fired.

HOWITZERS

Howitzers were shorter and lighter than field cannons and had a shorter range. They fired in an upward direction. This allowed the shell to fly over U.S. troops or battlefield obstacles before reaching the enemy. A Howitzer's shells were hollow iron spheres filled with gunpowder. They had a fuse that was lit when the shell was fired. The shell would explode at a predetermined time, ideally on impact. The shards could travel as far as 250 feet (76.2 m) when the shell exploded, causing damage to a wide area. Some howitzers also fired canisters filled with lead bullets. When fired, the canister disintegrated, spraying a shower of bullets at soldiers advancing on the gun's position.

Timeline

The War on the Battlefield

August 19, 1812
The USS *Constitution* defeats the British ship HMS *Guerriere* in the North Atlantic.

April 27, 1813
American forces capture York, or present-day Toronto. They burn the Legislative Assembly and other buildings.

July 12, 1812
General Hull leads the U.S. Army across the Detroit River into Canada.

October 13, 1812
The U.S. Army is defeated at the Battle of Queenston Heights in Ontario.

The War at Home

July 1, 1812
The United States doubles customs duties to fund the war.

June 18, 1812
The United States declares war on Great Britain.

September 10, 1813
The Americans, under Commodore Oliver Hazard Perry, win the Battle of Lake Erie, ending British naval control of the Great Lakes.

August 24, 1814
The British attack Washington, DC, setting the White House, Capitol, and other public buildings on fire.

October 5, 1813
At the Battle of the Thames, U.S. forces defeat the British and their American Indian allies. Tecumseh is killed in the battle, and the alliance of American Indian groups in the Northwest collapses.

July 5, 1814
The Americans win the Battle of Chippawa near Niagara Falls.

January 8, 1815
Unaware that the peace treaty had been signed, the United States defeats British forces at the Battle of New Orleans.

December 24, 1814
Great Britain and the United States sign the **Treaty** of Ghent, ending the war.

February 16, 1815
The Senate unanimously **ratifies** the Treaty of Ghent.

Key Battles

The War of 1812 took place in three main areas. The border region between Canada and the United States, along the St. Lawrence River and the Great Lakes, was a key battle zone as U.S. forces fought to take possession of the British holdings in the north. In the south, U.S. forces fought Great Britain's American Indian allies and defended New Orleans against British attack. At sea, American and British warships attacked each other's merchant fleets. The British also blockaded the American Atlantic coast.

The Battle of Lake Erie separated the British at Fort Amherstburg from their supplies. They had no choice but to abandon the fort and leave the area.

Battle of the Thames

The Battle of the Thames took place on October 5, 1813, in Upper Canada, now known as southern Ontario. After the British had captured the city of Detroit in August 1812, U.S. efforts were focused on recapturing it. They had managed to gain control of Lake Erie by September 1813 and had forced the British at Upper Canada's Fort Amherstburg from the area. This victory provided Major General William Henry Harrison with the opportunity to recapture Detroit.

Once this goal was achieved, Harrison and an army of about 3,700 men decided to pursue the British forces. The British, led by Major General Henry Procter, and their American Indian allies, led by Tecumseh, had fled to Moraviantown, a small American Indian settlement near the Thames River. Knowing that the U.S. forces were approaching, Procter began preparing his men and allies for battle.

SEPTEMBER 27

Fearing a U.S. attack, Major General Henry Procter leads his men and American Indian allies on a retreat from Fort Amherstburg to get supplies.

OCTOBER 2

With Detroit secured and **garrisons** set up to defend the area, Major General Harrison sets out in pursuit of Procter and his forces.

Harrison arrived the next day and ordered the cavalry to attack the main British line. The British were quickly overwhelmed, and their lone cannon was captured. Procter fled with about 250 men, and the rest of the British soldiers surrendered. The U.S. forces then turned their attention to the American Indian warriors. The fighting was fierce, and by the time it was over, Tecumseh was dead.

As news spread of Tecumseh's death, the American Indians retreated. They fled into the woods but were pursued by the American cavalry. The U.S. forces also burned Moraviantown, although the American Indians there had not been part of the fighting. With victory secured and Procter's army destroyed, Harrison returned to Detroit.

Tecumseh was killed by a gunshot wound to the chest. A number of people took credit for his death, but their claims could not be proven.

After their victory at the Battle of the Thames, the Americans controlled the Northwest frontier region for the rest of the war. Procter was later **court martialed** by the British Army for his actions during the battle. The death of Tecumseh was also significant. Without his leadership, the alliances that he had built with other American Indian groups collapsed, and the American Indians in the area were no longer a threat.

OCTOBER 4

Sensing that U.S. forces are closing in on his army, Procter stops near Moraviantown and prepares his men and allies for battle.

OCTOBER 5

The U.S. forces overpower the British at Moraviantown. The British either retreat or surrender. During the battle, Tecumseh is killed.

Battle of Chippawa

The Battle of Chippawa took place near the Niagara River during the American invasion of Upper Canada on July 5, 1814. At the time, Great Britain's war with Napoleon in Europe was coming to an end. Veteran British soldiers with battle experience were about to be sent to Canada, and the United States hoped to defeat the British before these reinforcements arrived. After suffering recent defeats in the war, the U.S. Army appointed several new commanders, including Jacob Brown and Winfield Scott.

U.S. forces occupied Fort Erie until November 1814, when they withdrew to Buffalo, New York. The fort is now a national historic site in Canada.

Brown commanded the Left Division of the Army of the North and planned to attack the main British base in Kingston, Ontario. A diversionary attack by militia was also planned to cross the Niagara River. When Brown could not get the support of the U.S. fleet on Lake Ontario, he decided to make the operation at Niagara his main attack. Brown crossed the river and captured Fort Erie on July 3. He then instructed Scott to move his forces to the north. While in transit, Scott's troops encountered a British force commanded by Major General Phineas Riall at Chippawa Creek. The two sides exchanged fire before Scott withdrew a short distance to the south.

JULY 3

Jacob Brown focuses his attention on crossing the Niagara River and securing lands on the other side. He leads his forces across the Niagara River and captures Fort Erie.

JULY 4

Brown instructs Winfield Scott to move his forces north to Chippawa Creek. Scott encounters British troops, who delay his advance.

Riall thought that Fort Erie was still in British hands and set out to relieve the defenders there on July 5. Early in the morning, his scouts and American Indian allies exchanged fire with some of the American outposts. Scott sent soldiers to help, but the U.S. troops were forced to retreat when they saw Riall's main force approaching.

By this time, Scott's troops had advanced to within range of the British. When Scott opened fire, the British replied with their own guns. Hoping to end the battle quickly, Riall ordered his men to surge toward the Americans. This opened a gap on the British right flank, and Scott saw his chance. Advancing both wings of his forces, his troops formed a U-shape and were able to fire on the British from three sides. The two armies were very close together and fired repeatedly for about 25 minutes before Riall ordered a retreat. The victory did much to raise morale among the U.S. forces. It proved to the soldiers, and the country as a whole, that U.S. soldiers could fight and win against a more experienced British Army.

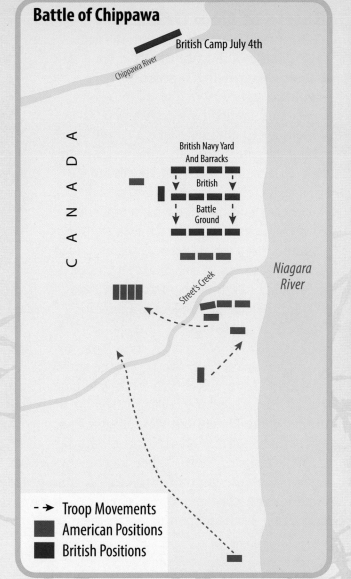

Battle of Chippawa

British Camp July 4th

Chippawa River

CANADA

British Navy Yard And Barracks

British

Battle Ground

Street's Creek

Niagara River

- ➤ Troop Movements
◼ American Positions
◼ British Positions

JULY 5

British Major General Phineas Riall heads toward Fort Erie to provide reinforcements, believing that the fort is still in British hands.

JULY 5

Scott fires upon Riall's forces. The British return fire, but are unable to gain ground. After about 25 minutes of fighting, the British retreat.

Battle of New Orleans

The Battle of New Orleans was the last major battle of the War of 1812. The British, unaware that a peace treaty had been signed, sent a naval invasion force commanded by Vice Admiral Sir Alexander Cochrane to attack New Orleans. Cochrane's fleet arrived off the coast of the city on December 12, 1814, with more than 8,000 men. Approximately 4,000 Americans commanded by Major General Andrew Jackson defended the city, while Commodore Daniel Patterson commanded U.S. Navy forces in the area. Patterson positioned his ships to guard the waters around the city, giving Jackson time to organize his defenses.

To counter the British attack on New Orleans, Jackson gathered a force of soldiers, locals, privateers, and black volunteers.

Cochrane was able to overpower the smaller U.S. fleet. Soon, the British forces had landed and established a base at Pea Island. They then marched inland and made camp at the Villere Plantation. Jackson sent troops to attack the camp, but the British stood firm, and U.S. forces withdrew to set up **defensive positions** at the Rodriguez Canal. When Lieutenant General Sir Edward Pakenham arrived with the main British force on January 1, 1815, he was angry that the Americans had been allowed to make such strong defenses. The two sides spent two weeks preparing for the main battle.

DECEMBER 12

Vice Admiral Alexander Cochrane's fleet arrives off the coast of New Orleans, with more than 8,000 men. They prepare for attack.

DECEMBER 23

After the victory at sea, British advance troops land and begin making their way inland. They set up camp at Villere Plantation.

Pakenham planned to advance on both sides of the river and launched his attack on January 8. It was a foggy day, and Pakenham's men marched straight into Jackson's artillery fire. Pakenham attempted to rally his men to continue the attack. He was wounded twice, and two horses were shot dead under him before a third wound led to his death on the battlefield. Other British commanders were also killed or wounded. British Major General John Lambert led the reserves forward, but they met the survivors of the main British forces as they were retreating. Lambert realized that the battle was lost and withdrew his troops.

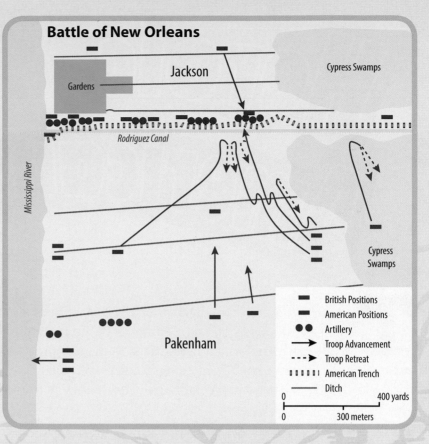

Battle of New Orleans

Jackson

Cypress Swamps

Gardens

Mississippi River

Rodriguez Canal

Cypress Swamps

Pakenham

▬	British Positions
▪	American Positions
●●	Artillery
→	Troop Advancement
---▶	Troop Retreat
▮▮▮▮	American Trench
—	Ditch

0   400 yards
0   300 meters

The Battle of New Orleans was the greatest American land victory of the war, against some of the finest soldiers in the British Army. Three British generals and eight colonels were killed during the battle. There were almost 2,500 British **casualties** during the campaign, compared to only about 300 American casualties. Weeks later, word reached both sides that the war had ended on December 24.

JANUARY 1

The main British force arrives, led by General Edward Pakenham. Both sides spend two weeks preparing for battle.

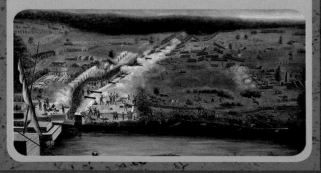

JANUARY 8

The British launch their attack, but are soon defeated. British reserves arrive but decide to withdraw when they realize the battle has already been lost.

Heroic Americans

The men who served in the War of 1812 came from a range of backgrounds. They shared a common desire to fight for their country. While many performed heroic acts, as the war progressed, some names became better known than others. Some soldiers were hailed for their bravery and strong leadership. Others were celebrated because they performed feats unlike anyone else.

Andrew Jackson
(1767–1845)

Andrew Jackson was one of the leading American commanders in the War of 1812. He also served as president of the United States from 1829 to 1837.

Jackson was born in the Carolinas in 1767. During the American Revolutionary War, he served as a messenger for the militia and spent time as a British prisoner. After the war, Jackson moved to Tennessee and became a lawyer. In 1796, he became Tennessee's first member of the U.S. House of Representatives. He served as a senator for a year and then as a judge on the Tennessee Supreme Court.

Jackson began his military career with the state militia and served as a major general in the War of 1812. He commanded U.S. forces against Great Britain's American Indian allies and defeated the British at the Battle of New Orleans in early 1815.

Jackson lost the presidential election in 1824, but won four years later. He left office in 1837 and retired to Tennessee. Jackson died in 1845, at the age of 78.

William Henry Harrison
(1773–1841)

William Henry Harrison served as a U.S. general in the War of 1812. He was later elected as the ninth president of the United States.

Harrison was born in Charles City County, Virginia, in 1773. He originally trained to be a doctor, but did not complete his studies and later joined the U.S. Army. He was involved in the Indian wars in the **Northwest Territory**. Harrison left the army in 1798 to enter politics. He held a number of posts, including governor of the new Indiana Territory.

Harrison rejoined the army at the start of the War of 1812. He was appointed as commander of the Army of the Northwest and recaptured Detroit from the British. He then defeated the British and their American Indian allies at the Battle of the Thames in 1813. After the war, Harrison lived in Ohio and served in the House of Representatives and the Senate. He was appointed the U.S. minister to Colombia in 1828. Harrison became U.S. president in March 1841, but died in Washington only 32 days after taking office, at the age of 68.

Jacob Brown
(1775–1828)

Jacob Brown was a commander in the New York Militia and U.S. Army during the War of 1812. He fought against British forces in Canada, winning several battles.

Brown was born in Bucks County, Pennsylvania, in 1775. He later moved to upstate New York, where he joined the New York Militia and rose to the rank of brigadier general. He then joined the U.S. Army, also as a brigadier general. At the Battle of Lundy's Lane, Brown was seriously wounded. The American forces retreated to Fort Erie, where Brown, although still injured, commanded his forces as they withstood a seven-week **siege**. The British eventually withdrew, and the Americans left the fort victorious.

When the war ended, Brown was a national hero. In 1821, he was appointed commander general of the U.S. Army. He held this position until his death in 1828 at the age of 52.

The Home Front

The War of 1812 mostly took place on battlefields and at sea, but it also had an effect away from the fighting. The British made their influence known throughout the United States. Blockades impacted the economy of the country, and the burning of the nation's capital was a strike to its very foundation. Some people questioned whether they were on the right side of the war. A few states even considered joining Canada. U.S. slaves and their families also took the opportunity to escape to Canada during the war. Many of the men fought on the British side once they had gained their freedom.

A Changing Economy

When the war started, Great Britain was the United States' main trading partner. The United States relied on the income generated from selling goods to Great Britain and was also dependent on Great Britain for supplying it with goods. The war brought this relationship to a halt, deeply affecting the economy of the United States. The British blockade of American waters also meant that the United States could not receive shipments from other countries. Many needed supplies became difficult to access as a result.

One key shortage was cotton cloth. The United States had cotton plantations but usually sent its cotton to Great Britain for manufacturing. As this was no longer possible, the United States had to find another way to access the cloth. The most efficient way was to make it themselves. In 1813, Francis Cabot Lowell, a Massachusetts merchant, set up a cotton manufacturing plant in the town of Waltham. The development brought the cotton shortage to an end and encouraged the development of similar industries in the North, helping the United States to become more economically self-sufficient.

Francis Cabot Lowell's cotton mill in Waltham was the first modern factory to be built in the United States. It was also the first factory in the United States to perform all stages of the manufacturing process.

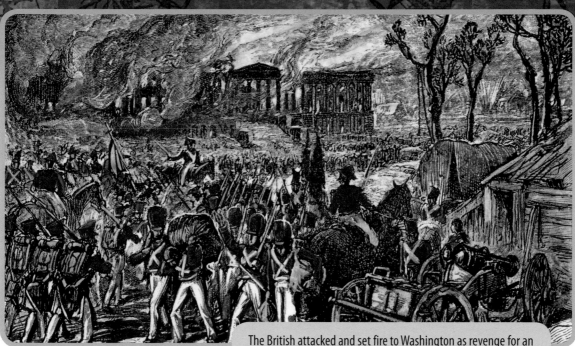

The British attacked and set fire to Washington as revenge for an American attack on the city of York at the beginning of the war.

The Burning of Washington

On August 24, 1814, the British Army attacked Washington and set fire to the city. Washington was relatively undefended as the British had already defeated its militia at the Battle of Bladensburg. Any remaining militia fled the city, knowing that they were seriously outnumbered. President Madison and government officials also escaped, along with their families. Sensing the panic, many residents rushed out of the city as well.

However, the British had been ordered to only target public buildings once Washington was captured. The **civilian** population was spared, but those who stayed watched as large parts of the city were burned. The White House, the uncompleted Capitol building, and several federal buildings were set on fire. Some private homes were also unintentionally destroyed as the flames spread. The House of Representatives and the Library of Congress were also burned before torrential rain put out the fires.

The British left the city two days later, realizing that they would not be able to maintain their control of it. When President Madison returned on August 27, he vowed to rebuild the city. The White House completed its restoration in 1817.

The Library of Congress had approximately 3,000 books at the time of the fire. All but one was lost to the fire.

New England

Many of the northern states, especially those close to the Canadian border, were firmly opposed to the war. The New England states were most affected by the loss of trade and the British blockade of the Atlantic coast. To restore their economic relationship with the British, these states began to discuss the benefits of leaving the United States and joining Canada.

The urge to fight the British subsided, and New Englanders began to look forward to contact with the enemy. In the final year of the war, the British Army occupied eastern Maine. The troops stationed there faced very little local opposition as the occupation gave local residents and merchants access to markets in New Brunswick and Nova Scotia. Other states shared similar sentiments. In Massachusetts, the governor even contacted the British about negotiating a separate peace.

Sir John Coape Sherbrooke was the British soldier responsible for staging the invasion of Maine. Following the takeover, he set up a government for the area.

At the end of 1814, **Federalist** delegates from the northeastern states met secretly at the Hartford Convention to discuss their issues regarding the war and trade. The Convention ended on January 5, 1815, and delegates went to Washington to discuss their grievances. However, by the time they arrived, the peace treaty had been signed. With the war at an end and trade channels reopened, New England decided against leaving the Union.

The Hartford Convention was held at the Old State House. Today, the building operates as a museum and learning center.

Not all African Americans sought to escape the United States. Some stayed to fight the British. The Louisiana Battalion of Free Men of Color fought under Andrew Jackson during the Battle of New Orleans.

Freeing of Slaves

At the time the war started, there were more than 1 million African American slaves in the United States. Many of them saw the War of 1812 as a chance to win their freedom. The British government made it clear that all slaves were officially free once they were safely under the rule of Great Britain. By 1813, slaves were making their way to the British ships blockading nearby waters and asking for refuge. In 1814, the British government began to encourage slaves to escape, offering them freedom if they reached a Royal Navy ship or managed to reach territory controlled by the British Army.

Thousands of slaves known as the Black Refugees escaped to freedom in the final two years of the War of 1812. Some of the men joined the British Army and fought in the campaign on the Atlantic coast. After the war, most of the former slaves resettled in Nova Scotia and New Brunswick, with a small number settling in Trinidad.

American slave owners suffered financial losses when their slaves escaped. Following American protests after the war, the British government agreed to pay more than $1 million to compensate those who had lost slaves.

The War Comes to an End

At various times during the war, both sides thought about opening negotiations for peace. These ideas, however, never moved forward. In April 1814, Napoleon was finally defeated, and Great Britain was able to turn its full attention to the situation in North America. With the end of the Napoleonic Wars came changes in Great Britain's needs. It no longer had to forcibly recruit American sailors. There was also no need to block U.S. trade with Europe. With two of the most contentious issues now moot, there was little reason to continue fighting. In August 1814, peace negotiations began at Ghent, a city in present-day Belgium. John Quincy Adams, who later served as president of the United States, led the American delegation.

At the time of the treaty signing, John Quincy Adams was serving as the ambassador to Russia.

Today, Ghent is located in Belgium. However, in 1814, its ownership was being disputed between France and the United Kingdom of the Netherlands.

The Battle of Plattsburgh was the last major British operation of the War of 1812, prior to the signing of the Treaty of Ghent. The British sent more than 11,000 troops into the battle to fight approximately the 4,000 American soldiers stationed at Plattsburgh.

The British came into the negotiations with several demands. First, they still wanted an American Indian state to be created in the Northwest Territory. They also demanded that there should be no U.S. naval forces on the Great Lakes and that Great Britain should have transit rights on the Mississippi River. In return, Americans could continue to fish off the coast of Newfoundland. The American delegation rejected the British demands, and negotiations stalled.

Back in the United States, the war continued. After attacking Washington, the British attempted to capture Baltimore. They were unsuccessful and were forced to withdraw from the area. In the north, 10,000 British troops invaded New York, but were defeated at the Battle of Plattsburgh on September 11. As negotiations continued in Ghent, another British invasion force was on its way to try to capture New Orleans.

The British eventually dropped their demands, and the two sides agreed on a treaty that did not involve any territorial changes. The Treaty of Ghent was signed in December 1814, but it took several weeks for the news to reach Washington. It was not until early March that all forces were aware of the war's end. It was only then that the fighting stopped.

Following the War of 1812, the relationship between the United States and Great Britain largely returned to that which had existed before the war. Trade resumed, and the two countries began relying on each other for various goods. However, the war did have an impact on the United States and its people. Although neither side could claim victory, Americans felt a great sense of national pride in the country's successes on the battlefields. Still, not everyone was able to return to their normal way of life. With Great Britain withdrawing its demand for an American Indian state, the end of the war had profound effects on the American Indians. In the years that followed, they were forcibly removed from their lands to make way for western expansion.

The Treaty of Ghent

The Treaty of Ghent was ratified by both the British and U.S. governments in February 1815. The treaty did not represent a victory for either side. Rather, it set the terms for the ceasefire. Both sides returned lands that had been captured. Great Britain gave back territory around the Great Lakes and in Maine. The United States returned lands it had taken in what is now the Canadian province of Ontario. All prisoners were released and allowed to return to their own country. Both sides returned all captured ships. The two countries also agreed to begin discussing the creation of a formal boundary between the United States and Canada and to work together to end the international slave trade.

American Nationhood

Even though neither side could claim victory in the War of 1812, there was one American success that could not be denied. The country had proven itself to be an independent country able to take on one of the greatest military powers in the world. Many Americans believed that Great Britain would never be able to control the United States again. This sense of national pride led to a period known as "the Era of Good Feelings," which lasted until the mid 1820s. Americans united in a common purpose for the good of the United States. With renewed optimism and empowerment, the country began making plans to continue its westward expansion, build up its military might, and improve its economic self-sufficiency.

The Erie Canal was one of the projects completed during the Era of Good Feelings. The canal provided an important transportation and trade route between New York City and Buffalo, New York.

American Indians

Following the signing of the Treaty of Ghent, Great Britain decided that it was in its best interest to maintain a solid relationship with the United States. As a result, it withdrew its championship of American Indian rights. Great Britain stopped supplying the American Indians with arms and removed itself from discussions regarding American Indian lands. The American Indians had to negotiate for themselves. Groups either reached agreements with the U.S. government and settlers, or they migrated farther west. When Andrew Jackson served as president in the 1830s, most of the American Indian groups in the southeastern United States were removed and sent to reservations west of the Mississippi. This displacement of American Indians would continue for decades to come.

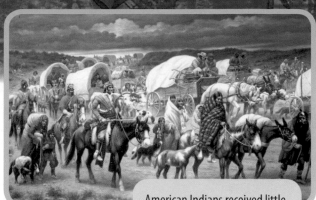

American Indians received little reward for their role in the War of 1812. Most were forcibly removed from their lands and placed on reservations to allow for more settlement.

THE STAR-SPANGLED BANNER

If the War of 1812 had not happened, *The Star-Spangled Banner* may not have become the U.S. national anthem. During the British attack on Fort McHenry in Baltimore on September 14, 1814, an oversized U.S. flag was raised over the fort. Francis Scott Key, an American lawyer and poet, saw the flag and began writing a poem. He based the poem on the melody of an old British song. The poem was originally called Defense of Fort McHenry but was later renamed *The Star-Spangled Banner*. The U.S. Navy began using the song for flag-raising ceremonies in 1889, and the army soon started using the song as well. In 1931, it became the country's official national anthem. The original flag is currently kept at the American Museum of National History in Washington, DC.

By The Numbers

Comparing Armies

When the War of 1812 began, the British Army had about 7,000 men, and the U.S. Army had about 12,000. By the time the war ended, each side had more than quadrupled its troop count.

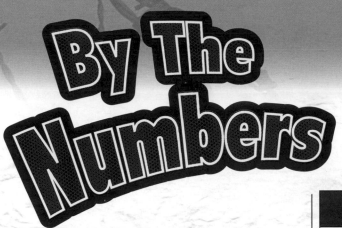

British Troops

United States Troops

👤 = 500 people

Men of the Militia

Not all men joined the U.S. Army. Many instead served with militia units from their own state or territory. Each area usually supplied men according to the size of its population. However, the number of men volunteering to fight was sometimes affected by whether or not the state or territory approved of the war with Great Britain.

Men of the Militia	
Connecticut	10,203
Delaware	3,838
District of Columbia	4,547
Georgia	11,557
Illinois Territory	2,357
Indiana Territory	3,380
Kentucky	20,239
Louisiana	9,687
Maryland	52,659
Massachusetts	46,681
Michigan Territory	556
Mississippi Territory	6,355
Missouri Territory	1,556
New Hampshire	5,955
New Jersey	6,012
New York	77,896
North Carolina	14,137
Ohio	24,521
Pennsylvania	29,317
Rhode Island	910
South Carolina	11,223
Tennessee	27,833
Vermont	5,236
Virginia	91,891

War Losses

The United States had more than 6,500 battle casualties during the War of 1812. The British had about 5,300. These numbers include only soldiers who were killed or wounded as a result of fighting. Many other soldiers lost their lives during the war. They died as a result of disease and illness caused by the conditions in which they lived.

American Troops

Wounded 69%

Killed 31%

British Troops

Wounded 70%

Killed 30%

The Cost of War

The War of 1812 was expensive for the United States. Raising an army and building weapons, ammunition, military equipment, and supplies all required major government funding. The amount of money needed was so large that the U.S. government had to borrow money from the **private sector** in order to maintain its forces.

American Military Spending
$95 million

Money Borrowed by
the United States
$82 million

Casualties of War

More than 2,000 Americans died in battle in the War of 1812, and more than 4,500 were wounded. While these numbers are only a portion of the casualties American soldiers experienced in other wars, they represent the nation's fight to reiterate its independence from its former mother country. This map indicates some of the war's key battles and the number of casualties on each side.

	Name of Conflict	United States Casualties	British Casualties
1	Queenston Heights	300	105
2	Thames	45	73
3	Lake Erie	123	135
4	Chippawa	299	469
5	New Orleans	71	2,037
6	Lundy's Lane	797	653
7	Baltimore	295	141
8	Plattsburg	220	388
9	Bladensburg	77	249
	Total	**2,227**	**4,250**

Legend

☐ United States

■ British Colonies

☐ Neutral

How We Remember

Many soldiers lost their lives as a result the War of 1812. Others returned home wounded. The war affected people all over the country. People wanted to honor those who had fought, those who had been injured, and those who had died throughout the course of the war.

THE CHALMETTE MONUMENT

The Chalmette Monument stands in the Chalmette Battlefield and National Cemetery of New Orleans. The monument was built to honor the soldiers who died during the Battle of New Orleans in January 1815. The monument is a 100-foot (30.5 m) tall **obelisk** that stands on a wide base with five steps. The obelisk has four corniced projections at the base, one of which serves a doorway to a spiral staircase. This leads to an observation chamber at the top of the obelisk. Construction of the monument began in 1855, but work was not completed until 1908.

BATTLE MONUMENT

Battle Monument is located in Baltimore's Battle Monument Square. The monument commemorates those who died in the Battle of Baltimore in September 1814. Representing the City of Baltimore, a statue of a female sits at the top of the monument. A crown of victory rests on her head, while her raised right hand holds a laurel wreath and her left hand hold a ship's rudder. A series of cords crisscross around the column. They are inscribed with the names of the men who died in battle.

PERRY'S VICTORY

Perry's Victory and International Peace Memorial in Put-in-Bay, Ohio, commemorates Commodore Oliver Hazard Perry's victory at the Siege of Fort Erie in September 1813. The memorial is also a symbol of the peace that prevailed between Great Britain, Canada, and the United States after the War of 1812. The memorial is 352 feet (107.3 m) tall and is made from 78 layers of pink granite. An 11-ton (10-metric-ton) bronze urn sits at the top of the column. The remains of three U.S. officers and three British officers who died in the battle are buried beneath the memorial's stone floor.

Memorials and other symbols of remembrance began to appear across the country in the decades after the war. These were local monuments, developed by individual communities, sometimes with assistance from the federal government. Today, these memorials and symbols continue to pay tribute to those who served in the War of 1812.

WAR OF 1812 MONUMENT

The War of 1812 Monument is located in Cannon Square in Stonington, Connecticut. The monument commemorates the defense of the city during shelling by British warships in August 1814. The attack damaged 40 buildings, but resulted in no deaths. The monument was built in 1830. It is made of granite and has a naval shell on the top. The monument is flanked by two recently restored 18-pound (8.2-kg) cannons. On the monument's south face is an inscription that lists the names of 10 residents who manned the cannons during the attack.

WELLS AND McCOMAS MONUMENT

The Wells and McComas Monument is located in Baltimore. It honors Daniel Wells and Henry McComas, two teenagers who were members of Captain Edward Aisquith's Militia Rifle Company in 1814. The boys are said to have killed British General Robert Ross on September 12, 1814, during the Battle of Baltimore. Ross had commanded the troops responsible for the burning of Washington a month earlier. Wells and McComas were also killed in the fighting in Baltimore. In 1854, the city decided to build a monument to commemorate the boys. Their bodies now lie under the monument's foundations.

OLIVER PERRY MONUMENT

The statue of Commodore Oliver Hazard Perry is located in Eisenhower Park in Newport, Rhode Island. The statue commemorates Perry's victory over the British in the Battle of Lake Erie. The statue is made of bronze and shows Perry with his left arm across his chest, holding the flag of the USS *Lawrence*. This had been his flagship before it was damaged during the battle and Perry transferred to the USS *Niagara*. The statue's right arm is raised, depicting Perry issuing commands on the ship. Perry's name is carved on the front of the statue, encircled by a wreath.

Test Yourself

MIX 'n MATCH

1. Robert Ross
2. USS Constitution
3. Tecumseh
4. Fort McHenry
5. Battle Monument
6. Oliver Hazard Perry
7. Shako

a. Battle of Lake Erie
b. *The Star-Spangled Banner*
c. Baltimore
d. Burning of Washington
e. HMS *Guerriere*
f. Shawnee
g. Hat

TRUE OR FALSE

1. Tecumseh was killed at the Battle of Chippawa.
2. The British Army burned the White House in Washington in August 1814.
3. William Henry Harrison only served as president for 32 days.
4. The Chalmette Monument is located in Washington.
5. The 1795 Springfield Infantry Musket was the main gun used by the U.S. Army.
6. Jacob Brown was a commander with the Northwest Territory Militia.
7. A howitzer was a field gun with a short barrel.
8. U.S. Army coats were mostly red.

MULTIPLE CHOICE

1. Who commanded the U.S. forces at the Battle of New Orleans?
   a. James Madison
   b. William Hull
   c. Andrew Jackson
   d. Jacob Brown

2. How many sailors were in the U.S. Navy in 1812?
   a. 2,500
   b. 5,000
   c. 10,000
   d. 15,000

3. What was the forced recruitment of sailors into the Royal Navy called?
   a. Blockade
   b. Impressment
   c. Annex
   d. Embargo

4. What was the name of the treaty that ended the war?
   a. The Treaty of Washington
   b. The Treaty of Ghent
   c. The Treaty of Paris
   d. The Treaty of Baltimore

5. Who led the American delegation in the treaty negotiations?
   a. John Quincy Adams
   b. William Henry Harrison
   c. Andrew Jackson
   d. James Madison

6. Which battle was the last major British operation before the treaty signing?
   a. Battle of Plattsburgh
   b. Battle of Chippawa
   c. Battle of New Orleans
   d. Battle of the Thames

7. Who composed the lyrics to *The Star-Spangled Banner*?
   a. Mary Pickersgill
   b. Winfield Scott
   c. Daniel Patterson
   d. Francis Scott Key

Answers:
Mix and Match
1. d. 2. e 3. f 4. b 5. c 6. a 7. g
True or False
1. False 2. True 3. True 4. True 5. False 6. True 7. True 8. False
Multiple choice: 1. c 2. b 3. b 4. b 5. a 6. a 7. d

Key Words

ally: a person or group who is associated with another for a common purpose

artillery: large caliber weapons, such as cannons and howitzers

Barbary War: one of two wars fought between the United States and the Barbary Islands of northern Africa in the 18th and 19th centuries

blockades: the isolation of an area, usually a port, by ships to prevent entry and exit

casualties: people who have been killed or wounded

civilian: a person who is not a member of the military

colonial rule: areas that are under the control of another country

Continental Congress: the assembly of delegates from the American colonies held during and after the War of American Independence

court martialed: tried in a court according to military law

customs duties: taxes put on imported goods

defensive positions: the placement of troops to withstand or deter attack

deserters: people who leave the military with no intention of returning

dictators: people who rule absolutely and oppressively

dragoon: a mounted infantryman

Federalist: a member of a major political party in the early years of the United States that wanted a strong central government

gaiters: a cloth or leather covering extending from the instep to the ankle or knee

garrisons: troops stationed in a fortified place

infantry: an army consisting of soldiers who fight on foot

Northwest Territory: the region north of the Ohio River, organized by Congress in 1787, comprising present-day Ohio, Indiana, Illinois, Michigan, Wisconsin, and the eastern part of Minnesota

obelisk: a tall, four-sided shaft of stone that has a pointed pyramid on the top

offensive: an attack launched by military forces against the enemy

private sector: the part of national economy run by private individuals or groups

ratifies: signs or gives formal consent to

regiment: a military unit that is usually made up of several large groups of soldiers

repeal: to officially make no longer valid

siege: when an army surrounds a city, town, or fortress in an attempt to capture it

sovereignty: complete independence and self-government

treaty: a document between two or more countries to agree to cooperate on certain matters. A treaty is also signed to agree on peace terms after a war is over.

Index

Log on to www.av2books.com

AV² by Weigl brings you media enhanced books that support active learning. Go to www.av2books.com, and enter the special code found on page 2 of this book. You will gain access to enriched and enhanced content that supplements and complements this book. Content includes video, audio, weblinks, quizzes, a slide show, and activities.

AV² Online Navigation

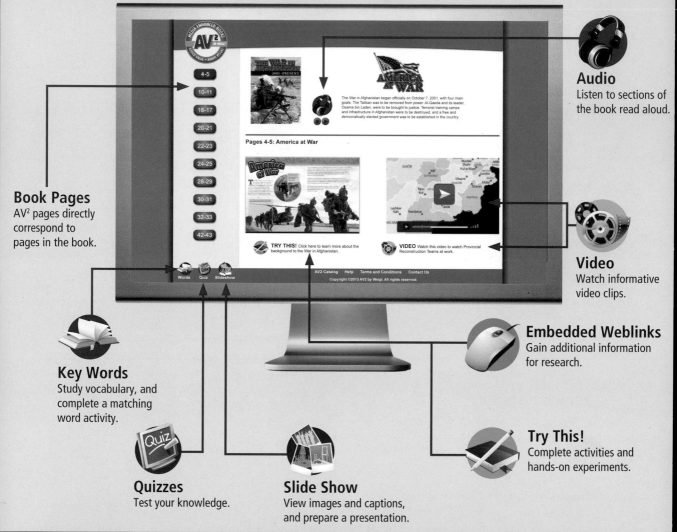

Book Pages
AV² pages directly correspond to pages in the book.

Key Words
Study vocabulary, and complete a matching word activity.

Quizzes
Test your knowledge.

Slide Show
View images and captions, and prepare a presentation.

Audio
Listen to sections of the book read aloud.

Video
Watch informative video clips.

Embedded Weblinks
Gain additional information for research.

Try This!
Complete activities and hands-on experiments.

AV² was built to bridge the gap between print and digital. We encourage you to tell us what you like and what you want to see in the future.

Sign up to be an AV² Ambassador at www.av2books.com/ambassador.